From Amazon Return Pallets to Resale Riches

The Ultimate Guide to Make Money Buying and Selling Amazon Liquidation Pallets

Hardeboyle Zain

date, and reliable, complete information. No warranties of any kind are declared or implied. Readers acknowledge that the author is not engaging in the rendering of legal, financial, medical or professional advice. The content within this book has been derived from various sources. Please consult a licensed professional before attempting any techniques outlined in this book.

By reading this document, the reader agrees that under no circumstances is the author responsible for any losses, direct or indirect, which are incurred as a result of the use of the information contained within this document, including, but not limited to, errors, omissions, or inaccuracies

TABLE OF CONTENTS

Introduction

Smart entrepreneurs and resellers searching for an efficient way to source inventory are becoming more and more fascinated with Amazon return pallets. These pallets are returned goods that were purchased by customers from Amazon but were later returned by them for a variety of reasons. Because of this, Amazon liquidates these goods in large quantities and sells them to resellers for a small fraction of their retail price.

"From Amazon Returns to Resale Riches: The Ultimate Guide to Buying and Selling Pallets" aims to give a thorough overview of the world of purchasing and selling Amazon return pallets. This guide will provide you with the information and resources you need to succeed, whether you're an experienced reseller or a newbie searching for a profitable side business.

In the sections that follow, we'll go over the advantages and risks of buying and selling Amazon return pallets, as well as offer advice on how to locate reputable suppliers, inspect and sort stock, sell items to maximize profit, and manage inventory and cash flow. We'll also offer suggestions on how to build up your business for long-term success and how to avoid popular risks and mistakes.

We'll start by talking about the many kinds of items that can be found inside return pallets and the probable conditions of the items you can encounter. Then, we'll offer advice on how to locate trustworthy liquidation companies and bargain for rates and terms. After that, we'll talk about checking and sorting pallets to find high-value items and possible profit margins for you.

It's important to carefully evaluate sales channels, pricing structures, and marketing methods when selling Amazon return pallets. We'll offer guidance on how to approach these choices in order to secure maximum profitability. In addition, we'll go over cash flow management, inventory control, and tactics for reinvesting earnings in growing your business.

While purchasing and selling Amazon return pallets might be a lucrative business, there are risks involved. We'll go over common pitfalls, such as how to handle returned or defective goods, customer complaints, and dishonest suppliers. We'll conclude by offering advice on how to grow your business and make it to be at the next level.

You'll be well-equipped on how to buy and sell Amazon return pallets by the time you finish this guide. This book will provide you with the skills and information you need to succeed, whether your goal is to make a quick buck or establish a long-term business. Let's plunge right in and begin discovering the fascinating world of Amazon return pallets!

Explanation of Amazon return pallets

Amazon return pallets are a type of merchandise that is

returned by customers to Amazon. These pallets can contain a wide range of products, including electronics, home goods, toys, apparel, and more. Many retailers and resellers purchase Amazon return pallets to resell them to customers at a discounted price.

When a customer returns a product to Amazon, it goes through a rigorous inspection process to ensure that it meets Amazon's standards for resale. If the product is in good condition and can be resold, it is added to a pallet of other returned products. These pallets are then sold to liquidators, who purchase them in bulk at a discounted price. Liquidators then sort through the products, grade them based on their condition, and sell them to retailers or resellers.

The condition of the products in an Amazon return pallet can vary widely. Some products may be new and unused, while others may have been opened and returned after minimal use. Some products may have cosmetic damage, while others may have functional issues. It is up to the liquidator to grade the products and provide a detailed description of their condition to potential buyers.

Retailers and resellers who purchase Amazon return pallets can save a significant amount of money compared to buying new products directly from manufacturers or distributors. However, they must be prepared to sort through the products and deal with any issues that may arise, such as damaged or defective items.

It is important to note that not all Amazon return pallets are the same. Some pallets may contain mostly electronics, while others may contain mostly clothing or home goods. It is important for buyers to research the products that are included in a particular pallet to ensure that it is a good fit for their business.

In conclusion, Amazon return pallets are a type of merchandise that is returned by customers to Amazon and then sold in bulk to liquidators. These pallets can contain a wide range of products in varying conditions and can be a cost-effective way for retailers and resellers to source inventory. However, buyers must be prepared to sort through the products and deal with any issues that may arise.

Benefits of buying and selling Amazon return pallets

For those who are prepared to put in the time and effort to thoroughly look through and assess the products, buying and selling Amazon return pallets may be a lucrative business. Here are some of the perks of purchasing and selling Amazon return pallets:

Low Cost: The low cost of buying and selling Amazon return pallets is one of its main advantages. These pallets are often bought in bulk by liquidators at a lower cost, enabling resellers to buy goods for a fraction of the price of purchasing new inventory straight from production companies or distributors.

Variety: A wide range of products, including electronics, home goods, toys, and more, can be found in Amazon return pallets. This variety enables resellers to provide their clients with a wide range of items.

High Profit Margin Potential: Resellers have the potential to make high profit margins by buying Amazon return pallets at a fraction of the original price and reselling them. This is particularly true for goods that may be sold for a high price and are in high demand.

Sustainability: Resellers are assisting in waste reduction and promoting sustainability by buying and re-selling Amazon return pallets. These products are being reused and sold to people who can use them rather than ending up in landfills.

Opportunities for Small Business Owners: For small business owners looking to start out in the reselling business, purchasing and selling Amazon return pallets can become a fantastic option. It can be a good strategy to create a prosperous business because of the low startup expenses and potential for huge earnings.

Flexibility in working hours and location is possible when reselling Amazon return pallets. Resellers can operate this business on their own schedules and from a home office or a small warehouse.

It is significant to note that there are risks associated with purchasing and selling Amazon return pallets. Resellers must be ready to handle consumer returns and refunds in the event that products are damaged or defective. Resellers can, however, reduce these risks and increase the advantages of this business model by conducting adequate research and product evaluation.

As a result, purchasing and reselling return pallets from Amazon can be a successful and long-lasting business model with minimal startup expenses and significant potential for profit. For those running a small business or seeking a flexible schedule, this could be a fantastic opportunity. Resellers contribute to trash reduction and sustainability by acquiring and reselling these goods.

Understanding Amazon Return Pallets

Types of products found in return pallets

It's important to be aware of the potential products you may run into when purchasing Amazon return pallets. It is essential to carefully evaluate each pallet before buying because return pallets frequently include a mixture of new, used, restored, and damaged products. We'll look at the many products that can be found in return pallets in this section.

Electronics and Appliances: Electronics and appliances, such as laptops, TVs, game consoles, tablets, smartphones, and small kitchen equipment, are frequently found in return pallets. These products may be new, used, or in several other situations. Despite the fact that they can be very profitable, it is crucial to carefully examine them to ensure all of the necessary parts are present and working.

Home Goods and Furniture: In addition to clothing, curtains, lamps, and chairs, return pallets may also contain home furnishings. These products can be brand-new or worn, and they could need to be cleaned or refurbished before being sold again. Despite the fact that they might be profitable, it's crucial to account for the extra expenses for maintenance and cleaning.

Clothes and Accessories: Items like shoes, purses, jewelry, and clothing are frequently included in return pallets under the clothing and accessories product category. These products may need additional cleaning or repairs before being resold and can either be brand-new with tags or used. It's critical to thoroughly check clothing items for marks, tears, and wear indications.

Return pallets may also include **toys and games**, including video games, puzzles, board games, and action figures.

These products can be brand-new or used, and they might need to be tested or repaired before being sold again. It's crucial to confirm that every component is there and in functional order.

Cosmetics, skincare products, and other items for personal care may be included in return pallets under the category of **health and beauty**. The condition of these items, which can be either new or used, must be checked before they are sold again to make sure they have not expired or damaged.

In conclusion, return pallets may include a variety of goods, thus it's crucial to thoroughly scrutinize each pallet before buying. Even though these items have a high potential for profit, it's crucial to account for the additional costs associated with cleaning, repairing, and testing. Purchasing Amazon return pallets may be a successful and satisfying business endeavor with a keen eye and some expertise.

Condition of items in return pallets

When buying Amazon return pallets, it's important to understand the condition of the items you may encounter.

Return pallets often contain a mix of new, used, refurbished, and damaged items, making it crucial to carefully inspect each pallet before making a purchase. In this section, we'll explore the different conditions of items you may find in return pallets.

New items

New items are products that have not been opened or used by a customer. These items are often found in return pallets when the original packaging is damaged or the customer returns the item for a different reason. New items are typically the most desirable type of product to find in a return pallet as they require little to no refurbishing or repair and can often be resold for close to their original retail value.

Used items

Used items are products that have been opened and used by a customer, but are still in working condition. These items may show signs of wear or use, but are still functional and may have some resale value. Used items are often sold at a lower price point than new items and may require additional cleaning or refurbishing before being resold.

Refurbished items

Refurbished items are products that have been repaired or restored to their original working condition. These items may have been returned by a customer due to a defect or issue that has since been resolved. Refurbished items are often sold at a lower price point than new items, but can still have a high resale value if they have been properly refurbished and tested.

Damaged items

Damaged items are products that have some level of damage or defect that makes them unsellable in their current condition. These items may have scratches, dents, missing parts, or other types of damage. Damaged items are often sold at a very low price point and may require significant refurbishing or repair before they can be resold.

In summary, the condition of items found in return pallets can vary greatly, from new items in perfect condition to heavily damaged items that require significant repair. It's important to carefully inspect each item in a pallet to determine its condition and resale value and to factor in the cost of any necessary refurbishing or repair. By understanding the different conditions of items found in return pallets, resellers can make informed decisions about which pallets to purchase and how to fully maximize their profits.

Potential profits and risks

For individuals who are aware of the possible rewards and risks, buying and selling Amazon return pallets can be a successful business enterprise. The benefits and drawbacks of purchasing and reselling return pallets will be discussed in this section.

Possible Profits:

Low Purchase Price: The low purchase price of return pallets is the main potential source of profit. Due to their combination of new, used, reconditioned, and damaged goods, pallets are sometimes sold at a discount. This makes it possible for resellers to get things in huge quantities for cheap.

High Resale Value: A lot of the products found in return pallets can be sold for more money than they cost to buy. This enables resellers to have substantial products on the money invested in the purchase of the products.

Recurring Customers: Resellers can have customers that keep buying more by providing high-quality items at competitive prices. Over time, this may result in more returning customers and more profits.

Flexibility: Resellers can operate from home and on their own schedule by purchasing and selling return pallets. This gives resellers flexibility and enables them to pursue additional business options.

Possible risks:

Quality Control: The items' quality control is one of the major issues associated with purchasing return pallets. It's crucial to properly inspect every item before reselling it because they can be broken, faulty, or missing pieces.

Extra Costs: The price of refurbishing and repairs can quickly rise, particularly if the products need extensive cleaning or repairs. Profits may be reduced as a result, which will make it harder to recover your investment.

Market competition: If there are too many resellers on the return pallet market, it may be challenging for resellers to offer their products at a profitable pricing range.

Limited Knowledge: Resellers may not be aware of the resale value of specific items or the costs associated with repairing or refurbishing specific products, which can result in unprofitable acquisitions.

In conclusion, purchasing and selling Amazon return pallets can be a successful business endeavor, but there are risks involved. When making a purchase, it's crucial to carefully examine each item and consider its possible resale value. Resellers should also take into account supplementary expenses like those for refurbishment and repairs, as well as be conscious of market rivalry. Resellers can have great profits in the return pallet market by making appropriate decisions and being aware of the risks and potential rewards involved.

Finding Reliable Sources of Amazon Return Pallets

How to find legitimate liquidation companies

Finding reputable liquidation companies that can offer you premium pallets at competitive prices is crucial if you're looking to purchase and sell Amazon return pallets. We'll look at some suggestions for locating reliable liquidation companies in this section.

Evaluate the company: To make sure a liquidation company is legitimate, do your homework on it before having any transaction with them. Visit their website to learn more about their background, experience, and customer feedback. Watch out for any warning signs, such as a website that lacks professionalism or lacks contact information or an actual address.

Verify certifications: Reputable liquidation businesses ought to have some kind of accreditation or certification. Consider choosing a company that is part of a group like the Better Business Bureau. You can be sure that you are conducting business with a trustworthy company because these organizations demand that businesses abide by particular standards and ethics.

Attend industry events: Meeting legitimate liquidation companies can be accomplished by attending industry events like trade shows and conferences. These gatherings offer the chance to speak with liquidation companies face-to-face, ask them questions, and inspect their merchandise in person. Also, you can network with other resellers to locate prospective business partners and gain insight into their experiences.

Request references: Request recommendations from other resellers who have conducted business with the liquidation company when evaluating them. Contact these references and find out their opinions on the business, the product's quality, and any difficulties they encountered. This can give important information about the company's credibility and dependability.

Begin with smaller orders: It's wise to start small when buying and selling Amazon return pallets to get a feel for the market. This will enable you to evaluate the pallets' quality and the company's quality of customer service before placing larger orders.

In conclusion, finding trustworthy liquidation companies is essential to the achievement of your goals as a reseller. You can make sure you're having business with a legitimate and dependable company that can offer you high-quality pallets at a fair price by doing your research, looking into the company's credentials, checking for certification, attending industry events, requesting references, and placing smaller orders at first.

Evaluating the reputation of potential suppliers

The reputation of your prospective suppliers might have a big impact on your business's success when it comes to purchasing Amazon return pallets. We'll look at some advice for assessing potential suppliers' reputations in this section.

Review customer testimonials: Reading customer testimonials is one of the most crucial steps in determining a potential supplier's reputation. Check for reviews on the vendor's website, social media, and independent review sites like Trustpilot or Google Reviews. To get a complete picture of the supplier's reputation, make sure to read both favorable and unfavorable reviews.

Check for certifications: Reputable suppliers frequently have accreditations or memberships in trade organizations that keep them to a certain standard. Search for suppliers who are affiliated with associations like the International Association of Resale Professionals or the National Retail Federation. These organizations frequently have stringent membership standards, which can give another layer of comfort that the supplier you are dealing with is reliable.

Examine their stock: Examine the supplier's inventory carefully to make sure they provide a wide range of products and that the state of those products is satisfactory. To ensure that the goods on the pallet are in good shape and will be profitable to resell, request images or a thorough description if at all possible.

Confirm the return policy: Before making a purchase, it's crucial to know the supplier's return policy. Reputable vendors ought to provide a transparent and equitable return policy that enables you to send back goods that are defective or not what was advertised. Watch out for vendors who strictly enforce no returns or who make it difficult to send back items.

Do your research on a possible **supplier's legal history** before working with them. Check if there are any pending lawsuits or complaints. Investigate the supplier's past for information regarding legal disputes, bankruptcies, or customer complaints. To find out if the supplier has been the subject of any complaints, contact your neighborhood BBB or consumer protection office.

Request references: Another useful method of assessing the supplier's reputation is to request recommendations from other resellers who have transacted with them. Ask these references about their interactions with the provider, the standard of the pallets, and any difficulties they encountered. This can give important information about the dependability and reputation of the supplier.

Assess supplier's communication and customer service: Consider how well the supplier communicates and treats customers. A trustworthy supplier should respond quickly to questions and give precise details about the goods and services they offer. They should be open and honest about their policies, prices, and return and refund policies. You may assess a supplier's dependability and trustworthiness by looking at their communication and customer service.

Have a look at the supplier's location: Take into account the supplier's location and any potential effects it may have on delivery times and shipping prices. If the supplier is far away from your business, you might have to pay more for transportation or wait longer for deliveries, which could affect your profits and customers ' satisfaction.

In conclusion, the success of your business as a reseller depends on how well you assess the reputation of possible suppliers. You can make sure you are doing business with a reputable and reliable supplier who can offer you high-quality pallets at an affordable price by checking customer reviews, checking for accreditation, checking their references, checking their inventory, checking their return policy, and considering their location.

Where to Find/Buy Amazon Return Pallets

As more and more consumers rely on online shopping for their needs, it's no surprise that Amazon has become one of the biggest names in the e-commerce industry. With millions of products sold every day, it's no wonder that there are also millions of returned items. While many of these items may be in perfectly good condition, Amazon simply can't sell them as new, leaving the company with an excess of returned inventory that they need to get rid of. This is where the opportunity for reselling Amazon return pallets comes in.

But from where specifically can you purchase these return pallets? There are several options to consider:

Directly from Amazon: Amazon has its own liquidation platform, Amazon Liquidation Auctions, where you can bid on and purchase Amazon return pallets. While this may seem like the most direct option, it's important to note that these auctions can be highly competitive, driving up prices and potentially lowering your profit margins.

Through liquidation companies: There are a number of third-party liquidation companies that work with Amazon and other major retailers to sell their returned inventory. These companies purchase large quantities of return pallets and then sell them to resellers at a lower cost. Some popular liquidation companies include B-Stock.com (For US/UK & EU), Direct Liquidation.com, and Liquidation.com.

Local auctions or liquidation stores: In some areas, there may be local auctions or liquidation stores that sell Amazon return pallets. These can be a good option if you prefer to inspect the pallets in person before purchasing and avoid shipping costs.

Wholesale Suppliers: Wholesale suppliers can also be an excellent source for buying Amazon return pallets. These suppliers may be able to offer bulk discounts and have more flexibility in the types of merchandise they offer. However, it's important to thoroughly vet any wholesale suppliers before doing business with them.

Online Marketplaces: Finally, online marketplaces such as eBay and Facebook Marketplace can be good sources for buying Amazon return pallets. However, buyers should be cautious when buying from individual sellers and thoroughly inspect the pallets before making a purchase.

Regardless of where you decide to buy Amazon return pallets, it's important to do your research and choose a reputable seller. Take the time to evaluate their reputation, inspect the pallets before purchasing, and negotiate prices and terms to ensure you're getting the best deal possible. With a bit of effort and determination, buying and reselling Amazon return pallets can be a profitable and rewarding business venture.

Negotiating prices and terms with suppliers

A key part of buying and selling Amazon return pallets is haggling over terms and prices with suppliers. Effective negotiation can help you get better deals and terms that will increase your revenue and overall business performance. We'll look at some advice on how to haggle over terms and prices with suppliers in this section.

Research is key: Before beginning any negotiation, it's crucial to carry out thorough research and gain a solid understanding of the market rates for the items you are considering. This will give you a place to start your discussions and assist you in determining what terms and a price are reasonable and fair.

Be ready to walk away: One of the best bargaining strategies is to be ready to leave if you can't come to an amicable agreement. This demonstrates to the supplier that you take your business seriously and that you will not put up with unfair conditions or prices.

Pay attention to value rather than just price: While price is a crucial consideration in any negotiation, it's also crucial to pay attention to the overall value that the supplier can offer. Think about factors like product quality, level of customer support, and supplier dependability. These aspects are frequently more significant than just the cost.

Be adaptable: As negotiation is a two-way process, be prepared to be adaptable and make concessions if doing so would result in a mutually beneficial agreement between you and the supplier. Think about several payment options, including a partial initial payment, or request a discount if you decide to buy more pallets.

Establish a relationship: A positive supplier relationship can help you get better terms and prices down the road. Be professional in your communication, make your payments on time, and give feedback on the grade of the goods you receive. By doing this, you can express to the supplier your appreciation for their services and your commitment to continuing your partnership.

In conclusion, bargaining with suppliers over terms and prices is a critical component of buying and selling Amazon return pallets. You may negotiate better rates and terms that can increase your profitability and overall business performance by doing your research, being ready to walk away, concentrating on value, being adaptable, and developing a strong relationship with your supplier.

Inspecting and Sorting Amazon Return Pallets

Importance of inspecting pallets before purchase

Inspecting pallets before purchase is a crucial step in buying and selling Amazon return pallets. Failing to inspect the pallets can result in receiving damaged or low-quality products, which can impact your reputation with customers and lead to financial losses. In this section, we'll explore the importance of inspecting pallets before purchase.

Identify damaged or expired products:

Inspecting pallets before purchase allows you to identify any damaged or expired products. This includes items with broken packaging, missing parts, or visible damage. By identifying these products, you can negotiate a lower price with the supplier or choose not to purchase the pallet altogether.

Assess product quality:

Inspecting pallets before purchase also allows you to assess the overall quality of the products. This includes checking for signs of wear and tear, rust, or other damage. By assessing the product quality, you can ensure that you are receiving high-quality products that are in good condition and can be resold at a fair price.

Assess potential profit:

By inspecting pallets before purchase, you can assess the potential profit that can be made from reselling the items included. This can include evaluating the average retail price of the items and comparing it to the purchase price of the pallet. Inspecting pallets before the purchase can help you make informed decisions about which pallets to buy and which to avoid based on the potential profit margins.

Ensure the accuracy of product description:

Inspecting pallets before purchase allows you to ensure the accuracy of the product description. This includes checking the product type, model number, and any other specifications. By ensuring the accuracy of the product description, you can avoid any misunderstandings or disputes with the supplier and ensure that you are receiving the products that you expect.

Protect your reputation:

Inspecting pallets before purchase is important for protecting your reputation with customers. By ensuring that you are receiving high-quality products, you can maintain customer trust and satisfaction, which can lead to repeat business and positive reviews.

Avoid financial losses:

Inspecting pallets before purchase is important for avoiding financial losses. By identifying damaged or low-quality products before purchase, you can avoid reselling them at a loss or having to dispose of them altogether. This can help protect your bottom line and ensure the long-term success of your business.

In conclusion, inspecting pallets before purchase is a crucial step in buying and selling Amazon return pallets. By identifying damaged or expired products, assessing product quality, ensuring the accuracy of the product description, protecting your reputation, and avoiding financial losses, you can ensure that you are receiving high-quality products that can be resold at a fair price.

Sorting products into categories

Sorting products into categories is an important step in the process of buying and selling Amazon return pallets. By organizing the products into categories, you can identify which items are in high demand, which ones may require additional marketing efforts, and which ones may need to be disposed of or sold at a discount. In this section, we'll explore the importance of sorting products into categories and some tips for doing so effectively.

Identify high-demand items:

Sorting products into categories allows you to identify

which items are in high demand and which ones are not. This can help you prioritize your efforts and focus on selling the items that are likely to generate the most profit. For example, electronics and home appliances are typically in high demand, while clothing and personal care items may require more marketing efforts to sell.

Streamline the listing process:

Sorting products into categories can help streamline the process of listing items for sale. By organizing items into groups based on their type or condition, you can create listings more efficiently and quickly. This can help you save time and focus on other aspects of your business.

Separate damaged items:

Sorting products into categories also allows you to separate any damaged or low-quality items from the rest. This can include items with broken parts, missing pieces, or signs of wear and tear. By separating these items, you can avoid selling them at full price and instead offer them at a discount or dispose of them if necessary.

Group items by type or brand:

Organizing products into categories by type or brand can help you identify trends and make informed decisions about future purchases. For example, grouping all electronic items together can help you identify which brands or types of electronics are most popular and which ones may need to be avoided in the future.

Consider expiration dates:

If you're selling items with expiration dates, such as food or personal care products, it's important to separate them into categories based on their expiration dates. This can help you avoid selling expired products and ensure that you're only selling items that are safe for use.

Improve the customer experience:

Organizing products into categories can also improve the customer experience when shopping on your website or marketplace. Customers can quickly and easily find what they are looking for, and they can browse related products in the same category. This can help increase customer satisfaction and encourage repeat purchases.

Profit maximization is another benefit of categorizing products. You can tell which goods are doing well and which ones aren't by classifying your products into different groups. This can assist you in making well-informed choices regarding the goods you'll buy in the future and the categories you should concentrate on. Also, you can engender a sense of urgency and scarcity by designating categories for high-demand goods, which can raise demand and result in higher costs.

Identify trends:

Sorting products into categories can also help you identify trends in the marketplace. By tracking which categories are selling well and which are not, you can identify shifts in consumer preferences and adjust your purchasing and selling strategies accordingly. This can help you stay ahead of the competition and maximize profits.

In conclusion, sorting products into categories is an important step in the process of buying and selling Amazon return pallets. By identifying high-demand items, separating damaged items, grouping items by type or brand, considering expiration dates, and making it easy for customers to navigate your inventory, you can make informed decisions about which items to sell and how to market them effectively.

Identifying high-value items and potential profit margins

Identifying high-value items and potential profit margins is crucial when buying and selling Amazon return pallets. By understanding which items are likely to generate the most profit, you can make informed decisions about which pallets to purchase and how to price your items. In this section, we'll explore some tips for identifying high-value items and calculating potential profit margins.

Identify high-value items by **researching the market demand** for various product categories. This is one of the first steps in the process. This can assist you in identifying the goods that are most likely to sell quickly and for a premium price. Electronics, appliances, and home goods, for instance, frequently have great demand, whereas apparel and personal care products could need more marketing support to be successful.

Pay attention to brand names:

Brand names can often be a sign of luxury items. Popular brands are frequently thought to be of greater quality and can thus be more expensive. It's crucial to remember that some brands could have a greater return rate than others, so before buying a pallet, it's necessary to look into the brand's reputation.

Check the condition of items:

The condition of items can also be a factor in determining their value. Items in like-new condition will likely command a higher price point than those with signs of wear and tear or missing parts. However, even items with some damage may still be sellable, especially if they can be repaired or sold at a discount.

Estimate repair or refurbishing costs:

If you come across damaged or broken items, it's important to estimate the repair or refurbishing costs before deciding whether to sell them. This can help you determine whether it's worth investing in repairs or if it's more cost-effective to sell the item at a discounted price or dispose of it altogether.

Consider potential profit margins:

When evaluating the value of items, it's important to consider the potential profit margins. This means calculating the difference between the purchase price of the pallet and the potential selling price of each item. Keep in mind that some items may require additional costs, such as repair costs or marketing expenses, which can affect the overall profit margin.

Look for unique or rare items:

Unique or rare items can also be high-value items, as they may appeal to collectors or niche markets. For example, vintage electronics or limited edition products may command a higher price point.

Assess competition:

Finally, it's important to assess the competition in the market. If there are many sellers offering the same product, it may be difficult to sell at a high price. However, if there is less competition, you may be able to sell the item at a higher price.

In conclusion, identifying high-value items and potential profit margins is an important part of the process of buying and selling Amazon return pallets. By researching market demand, looking for brand names, checking the condition of items, considering potential profit margins, knowing the level of competition, and looking for unique or rare items, you can make informed decisions about which items to sell and how to price them for maximum profit.

Selling Amazon Return Pallets

Choosing the right sales channels (online vs. in-person)

Once you have sorted and identified the high-value items in your Amazon return pallet, it's time to choose the right sales channels to sell your products. Two popular options for reselling Amazon return pallets are online marketplaces and in-person sales. In this section, we'll explore the advantages and disadvantages of each channel to help you make an informed decision.

1. Online Sales:

Online sales channels are the most popular way to sell

Amazon return pallets. The advantages of online sales are:

* Access to a large customer base: Online marketplaces like Amazon, eBay, and Facebook Marketplace have millions of active buyers. This gives you access to a large customer base and increases the chances of selling your products quickly.

* Lower overhead costs: Selling online eliminates the need for a physical storefront, which can significantly lower overhead costs. You don't need to pay for rent, utilities, or staff, which means that you can keep your prices competitive.

* Convenient and flexible: Online sales allow you to sell from anywhere, at any time. This means that you can run your business from the comfort of your home and set your schedule.

* Ability to target niche markets: Online marketplaces offer the ability to target specific customer segments, such as collectors or hobbyists. This can be an advantage if you

have unique or rare items in your Amazon return pallet.

However, there are also some disadvantages to selling online, including:

* High levels of competition exist in the internet market, making it challenging for merchants to stand out. To draw customers, you must put time and effort into your product marketing.

* Shipping and handling fees: For larger or heavier items, shipping and handling fees might be a substantial expense. When setting your product prices, you must take these expenses into account.

* Limited ability to inspect products: Online sales make it difficult to inspect products before purchase, which can lead to customer complaints or returns.

2. **In-person Sales:**

In-person sales channels include flea markets, garage sales, and consignment stores. The advantages of in-person sales are:

* Personal interaction with customers: In-person sales allow you to interact with customers face-to-face, which can build trust and increase sales.

* Ability to inspect products: In-person sales allow customers to inspect products before purchase, which can reduce the likelihood of complaints or returns.

* Opportunity for bargaining: In-person sales offer the opportunity for bargaining, which can increase the chances of selling your products quickly.

However, there are also some disadvantages to in-person sales, including:

* Limited customer reach: In-person sales have a limited customer reach, which can make it difficult to sell larger quantities of products quickly.

* Higher overhead costs: In-person sales require a physical storefront or booth, which can be expensive to rent or

purchase.

* Time-consuming: In-person sales can be time-consuming, as you need to set up your booth and attend the event.

In conclusion, both online and in-person sales channels have their advantages and disadvantages. The right choice depends on your business goals, the types of products you are selling, and your target customer base. To maximize your profits, consider a mix of both channels, and always factor in the costs and time associated with each option when making your decision.

Tips for pricing products for maximum profit

Pricing your products correctly is essential to maximize your profit when reselling Amazon return pallets. If your prices are too high, you may struggle to sell your products, but if they are too low, you risk leaving money on the table. In this section, we'll explore some tips for pricing your products for maximum profit.

Research the Market:

Before you price your products, it's essential to research the market and understand the price range for similar items. Check out online marketplaces, such as Amazon and eBay, to see how other sellers are pricing their products. This will give you a baseline for your prices and help you avoid overpricing or underpricing your products.

Factor in Your Costs:

When pricing your products, you need to factor in your costs, including the purchase price of the pallet, shipping, handling, and any fees associated with the sales channel you are using. Make sure you know your costs so that you can set a realistic price that covers your expenses and allows you to make a profit.

Consider the Condition of Your Products:

The condition of your products is a critical factor when pricing your items. Products that are brand new or in excellent condition can be priced higher than those that are used or damaged. Make sure you accurately describe the condition of your products and adjust your prices accordingly.

Determine Your Profit Margin:

To determine your profit margin, subtract your costs from the selling price of your products. Your profit margin will vary depending on the types of products you are selling and your target profit goals. Consider your target profit margin when setting your prices, and make sure you are pricing your products to achieve that goal.

Use Psychological Pricing Techniques:

Psychological pricing techniques, such as ending your prices with 9 or 5, can help you maximize your profits. Research shows that prices ending in 9 or 5 can make products appear more affordable and increase sales. Experiment with different pricing strategies to see what works best for your products.

Watch Your Competitors:

Keep an eye on the prices your rivals are charging and

change your own accordingly. You might need to change your prices if other sellers are setting their prices for their goods lower than yours in order to stay competitive. On the other hand, avoid underpricing your goods to the point that you are losing money.

In conclusion, pricing your products for maximum profit requires careful consideration of your costs, market research, and the condition of your products. Use psychological pricing techniques and monitor your competitors' prices to ensure you are pricing your products competitively while achieving your profit goals. By following these tips, you can set the right prices for your products and maximize your profits when reselling Amazon return pallets.

Marketing strategies for reaching potential customers

Once you have sorted and priced your products, the next step is to market them effectively to potential customers. Here are some marketing strategies for reaching potential customers when reselling Amazon return pallets:

Online Marketplaces: Online marketplaces, such as Amazon and eBay, are excellent platforms for selling your products. These marketplaces have a large customer base, and they handle payment processing and shipping for you, making it easy to sell your products. Make sure to optimize your product listings with clear descriptions, quality images, and competitive prices to attract potential customers.

Social media: Online communities and sites like Facebook and Instagram are excellent for spreading the word about your items and connecting with potential buyers. Make social media profiles for your business and use them to promote news and promotions, showcase your products, and interact with your followers. Also, you can advertise on social media to target particular demographics and increase traffic to your website's shop or product listings.

Email Marketing: It is an effective way to reach potential customers and promote your products. Collect email addresses from your website, social media accounts, and in-person sales, and send regular newsletters with updates on your products, promotions, and discounts. Use a professional email marketing service to create visually appealing emails and track your campaigns' effectiveness.

Influencer marketing: Partnering with social media influencers that have a sizable following to promote your products is known as influencer marketing. Find influencers who can connect with your target market and who have the same values as your business in your specialty or sector. To get them to advertise your products to their following, you might provide them with free products or a commission on purchases.

In-Person Sales: If you have a physical store or attend local markets or events, in-person sales can be an effective way to reach potential customers. Create eye-catching displays for your products and engage with customers to build rapport and promote your products. Offer special promotions or discounts for in-person sales to encourage customers to make a purchase.

In conclusion, effective marketing strategies are essential for reaching potential customers when reselling Amazon return pallets. Utilize online marketplaces, social media, email marketing, influencer marketing, and in-person sales to promote your products and reach your target audience. Experiment with different strategies and track your results to find what works best for your business. With the right marketing strategies, you can increase your sales and maximize your profits when reselling Amazon return pallets.

Managing Inventory and Cash Flow

Tips for keeping track of inventory

One of the most critical aspects of successfully reselling Amazon return pallets is keeping track of inventory. Here are some tips for effectively managing your inventory:

Use Inventory Management Software:

Invest in inventory management software that can help you keep track of your products, sales, and stock levels. These tools can help you automate your inventory management, save time, and prevent stockouts.

Label Your Products:

Labeling your products can help you keep track of your inventory and prevent mix-ups. Use a unique identifier, such as a SKU or barcode, for each product, and ensure that it is clearly visible on the packaging.

Conduct Regular Stocktakes:

Conduct regular stocktakes to ensure that your inventory records match your physical inventory. This can help you identify discrepancies and prevent stockouts. Use a checklist to ensure that you count all of your products accurately.

Categorize Your Products:

Categorize your products into different groups based on their sales velocity or profit margin. This can help you identify your best-selling products, slow-moving items, and products with high-profit margins. Use this information to adjust your pricing, marketing, and purchasing strategies accordingly.

Set Reorder Points:

Set reorder points for each product to ensure that you always have enough stock on hand. When your stock levels fall below the reorder point, you can order more products to prevent stockouts.

Use a First-In, First-Out (FIFO) System:

Implement a first-in, first-out (FIFO) system to ensure that you sell your oldest products first. This can help prevent stock losses due to expired or outdated products.

Track Returns and Refunds:

Track returns and refunds to ensure that you have an accurate record of your inventory levels. If a product is returned, make sure that it is inspected and tested before it is returned to inventory.

In conclusion, keeping track of your inventory is essential for successfully reselling Amazon return pallets. Use inventory management software, label your products, conduct regular stocktakes, categorize your products, set reorder points, use a FIFO system, and track returns and refunds to effectively manage your inventory. With these tips, you can prevent stockouts, reduce waste, and maximize your profits.

Strategies for reinvesting profits

Reinvesting profits is essential for growing your Amazon return pallet resale business. Here are some strategies for reinvesting your profits:

Purchase More Inventory:

One of the most straightforward strategies for reinvesting profits is to purchase more inventory. By reinvesting your profits into more inventory, you can increase your product selection, expand your customer base, and grow your revenue.

Expand Your Sales Channels:

Expanding your sales channels can help you reach more customers and increase your sales. Consider selling on additional online marketplaces, such as eBay or Facebook Marketplace, or opening a physical store.

Enhance Your Marketing:

Making an investment in marketing will help you attract new customers and boost sales. To increase your visibility and increase traffic to your website, think about investing in social media advertising, email marketing, or search engine optimization (SEO).

Upgrade Your Equipment and Tools:

Upgrading your equipment and tools can help you improve your productivity and efficiency, which can lead to increased profits. Consider investing in a better computer, barcode scanner, or label printer to speed up your processes and improve your accuracy.

Hire Assistance:

If you discover that fulfilling orders or performing administrative duties is taking up too much of your time, you might choose to hire assistance. Your time can be freed up so you can concentrate on expanding your business by hiring an employee or outsourcing some chores to a freelancer.

Expand Your Product Selection:

Expanding your product selection can help you attract more customers and increase your sales. Consider adding complementary products to your inventory, such as accessories or related items.

Pay Down Debt:

If you have outstanding debt, consider using your profits to pay it down. Paying down debt can help you reduce your interest expenses and improve your cash flow, which can help you reinvest in your business in the future.

In conclusion, reinvesting your profits is critical for growing your Amazon return pallet resale business. By purchasing more inventory, expanding your sales channels, improving your marketing, upgrading your equipment and tools, hiring help, expanding your product selection, or paying down debt, you can increase your revenue and profitability. Consider implementing one or more of these strategies to reinvest your profits and take your business to the next level.

Dealing with slow-moving products and inventory management

One of the biggest challenges that Amazon return pallet resellers face is dealing with slow-moving products. Slow-moving products are items that don't sell as quickly as expected, and they can tie up your cash flow and take up valuable warehouse space. Here are some tips for dealing with slow-moving products and inventory management:

Analyze Your Sales Data:

The first step in managing slow-moving products is to analyze your sales data. Look at your sales reports to identify which products are selling well and which ones are not. This will help you identify slow-moving products and develop a plan to address them.

Identify the Reasons for Slow Sales:

Once you've identified slow-moving products, try to figure out why they're not selling. Are they priced too high? Are they out of season? Do they have a defect or other issue that's deterring buyers? By understanding the reasons for slow sales, you can develop a plan to address the problem.

Adjust Your Pricing:

If your slow-moving products are priced too high, consider reducing the price to make them more attractive to buyers. You can also bundle slow-moving products with other products or offer discounts to encourage sales.

Liquidate Slow-Moving Products:

If you've tried adjusting your pricing and other strategies to increase sales, and the products are still not moving, consider liquidating them. You can sell them to a liquidator, donate them to a charity, or sell them at a deep discount to clear out your inventory and free up space for more profitable products.

Offer Discounts or Promotions:

Consider offering discounts or promotions on slow-moving products to stimulate demand. For example, you can offer a buy-one-get-one-free promotion or a percentage off the regular price. This can help you clear out slow-moving inventory and generate cash flow.

Improve Your Inventory Management:

Effective inventory management is essential for preventing slow-moving products from tying up your cash flow and taking up valuable warehouse space. Consider using inventory management software to track your inventory levels and sales data. This will help you identify slow-moving products and take action to address them before they become a problem.

Demand Prediction:

Predict demand for your products using data from your sales. You'll be better able to decide when and how much inventory to order as a result. By predicting demand, you may avoid overstocking items that don't sell well and concentrate on stocking popular items.

In conclusion, slow-moving products can be a challenge for Amazon return pallet resellers, but with the right strategies in place, you can manage your inventory effectively and maximize your profits. Analyze your sales data, identify the reasons for slow sales, adjust your pricing, liquidate slow-moving products, improve your inventory management, and forecast demand to manage slow-moving products effectively. By implementing these strategies, you can reduce your inventory costs, increase your cash flow, and maximize your profitability.

Avoiding Common Pitfalls and Risks

'Handling damaged or defective products

As an Amazon return pallet seller, it's important to have a plan in place for handling damaged or defective products. Dealing with these products can be challenging, but it's crucial to have a strategy in place to minimize the impact on your business. Here are some tips for handling damaged or defective products effectively:

Inspect Pallets Before Purchase:

One of the best ways to avoid purchasing damaged or defective products is to inspect them before you buy them.

Look for signs of damage or wear and tear, such as scratches, dents, or broken parts. You should also test electronic products to ensure that they are functioning properly.

Separate Damaged or Defective Products:

As you sort through your inventory, you may come across products that are damaged or defective. Set these products aside in a separate area of your warehouse so that you can deal with them later. This will help you avoid selling damaged or defective products to your customers.

Contact the Supplier:

If you receive a pallet with damaged or defective products, contact the supplier immediately. Explain the issue and provide evidence, such as photos or videos. Ask the supplier about their return policy and how they plan to resolve the issue. In some cases, the supplier may offer a refund or replacement for damaged or defective products.

Salvage and Repair Products:

In some cases, damaged or defective products can be salvaged and repaired. For example, you may be able to fix a broken electronic device or replace a missing part. Consider whether it's worth the time and effort to salvage the product and whether you can sell it at a profit.

Consider selling a **broken or defective product for components or scrap** if you are unable to salvage it. You can be able to recover part of your investment by offering useful parts or components for sale. It's important to note that selling products as pieces or parts may not be as lucrative as selling them in their original state.

Provide Replacements or Refunds: Whenever a customer purchases a faulty or damaged item, provide them with a refund or a replacement. By doing this, you may retain positive customer relations and steer clear of bad comments or reviews. In order to lessen the effect on your business, be ready to handle returns swiftly and effectively.

Donate or Dispose of Products:

If you're unable to salvage or sell a damaged or defective product, consider donating it to a charitable organization or disposing of it responsibly. Donating products can be a great way to give back to your community while minimizing waste. However, make sure to dispose of any hazardous or toxic materials in accordance with local regulations.

In conclusion, handling damaged or defective products can be a challenge for Amazon return pallet sellers. However, with proper inspection, communication with suppliers, and a solid plan for salvaging, selling, or disposing of damaged products, you can minimize the impact on your business. Remember to prioritize customer satisfaction and follow local regulations for disposing of hazardous or toxic materials.

Dealing with customer returns and complaints

Dealing with customer returns and complaints is an important aspect of selling Amazon return pallets. While you may take steps to minimize the number of returns and complaints, you will inevitably encounter some unhappy customers. Here are some tips for dealing with customer returns and complaints:

Have a Clear Return Policy:

One of the best ways to minimize customer returns and complaints is to have a clear return policy. Ensure your policy is easy to understand and prominently displayed on your website or store. Be sure to include information on how to return products, how long customers have to return products, and any restrictions or conditions.

Respond to Customer Complaints Quickly:

If a customer contacts you with a complaint, respond as quickly as possible. Make sure you listen carefully to their concerns and try to address their issues in a professional and empathetic manner. If possible, offer a solution that meets their needs and demonstrates your commitment to customer satisfaction.

Provide Refunds or Replacements:

Be ready to provide a refund or a replacement if a customer requests to return a product. Make sure your return handling procedure is well-defined and that you adhere to it regularly. Keep the customer abreast of any updates or changes by keeping in touch with them throughout the process.

Document Customer Complaints:

If you receive a customer complaint, be sure to document it. Keep a record of the complaint, the steps you took to address it, and the outcome. This can help you identify trends or recurring issues and improve your business processes.

Learn from Customer Feedback:

Customer feedback can be a valuable source of information that can help you improve your business. If you receive a complaint or negative feedback, take it as an opportunity to learn from your mistakes and make changes to your business practices.

Maintain a Professional Attitude:

Dealing with customer returns and complaints can be frustrating, but it's important to maintain a professional attitude at all times. Be patient and understanding with your customers, even if they are angry or upset. Remember that your goal is to resolve their issue and maintain good customer relations.

In conclusion, dealing with customer returns and complaints is an important aspect of selling Amazon return pallets. By having a clear return policy, responding to customer complaints quickly, offering refunds or replacements, documenting customer complaints, using customer feedback to improve, and maintaining a professional attitude, you can minimize the impact of returns and complaints on your business. By being proactive and transparent with your customers, you can maintain good customer relations and build a successful business selling Amazon return pallets.

Protecting against scams and fraudulent suppliers

It's crucial to safeguard oneself against con artists and

dishonest suppliers while buying and selling Amazon return pallets. Here are some pointers to assist you to stay clear of con artists and dishonest vendors:

Research the Supplier:

Before buying from a supplier, research their reputation and history. Look for reviews and feedback from other buyers, both online and offline. You can also check with organizations like the Better Business Bureau to see if there have been any complaints or legal actions against the supplier.

Check the Supplier's Credentials:

Make sure the supplier is licensed and registered with the appropriate authorities. You can also check their credit history and financial stability. If the supplier is unwilling to provide this information or there are discrepancies, it could be a sign of fraudulent activity.

Avoid Wire Transfers and Cash Payments:

Be cautious when paying for Amazon return pallets with

wire transfers or cash. These methods are more difficult to track and can leave you vulnerable to fraudulent activity. Use credit cards or other payment methods that offer protection and are easier to trace.

Watch Out for Unrealistic Promises:

Be wary of suppliers who promise unrealistic profits or guarantees of success. While buying and selling Amazon return pallets can be profitable, it's important to be realistic about the potential risks and challenges.

Inspect the Pallets Before Purchase:

Inspect the pallets before making a purchase. If possible, visit the supplier's warehouse to see the pallets in person. Look for signs of damage or tampering and make sure the products match the description provided by the supplier.

Use a Third-Party Escrow Service:

Consider employing a third-party escrow provider to safeguard your cash and lower the possibility of fraud. The buyer and the seller are both protected by these services since they hold the money until both parties have met their obligations.

Trust Your Gut:

If something looks too good to be true or if you have a terrible feeling about a source, follow your gut instinct and explore alternatives. Instead of taking the chance of losing money or harming your business ' reputation, it is best to remain careful and steer clear of any scams or fraudulent conduct.

In conclusion, protecting yourself against scams and fraudulent suppliers is essential when buying and selling Amazon return pallets. By researching the supplier, checking their credentials, avoiding wire transfers and cash payments, watching out for unrealistic promises, inspecting pallets before purchase, using a third-party escrow service, and trusting your gut, you can reduce the risk of fraudulent activity and protect your business from financial losses.

Scaling Up Your Amazon Return Pallet Business

Expanding your product range

Growing your Amazon return pallet business requires taking the crucial first step of expanding your product line. Here are some pointers for doing so:

Research Market Trends:

Before expanding your product range, it's important to research current market trends to identify potential opportunities. Look for product categories or niches in high demand or that align with your existing offerings.

Consider Customer Needs:

Another important consideration when expanding your product range is your customers' needs. Consider what products they are looking for and what would complement your current offerings. This can help you attract new customers and increase customer loyalty.

Source from Multiple Suppliers:

When expanding your product range, it's important to source from multiple suppliers to reduce your reliance on a single source. This can also help you find better deals and improve your bargaining power when negotiating prices and terms.

Test New Products:

Before committing to a new product line, consider testing it first to gauge its potential success. This can involve selling a small quantity of the product or offering it as a limited-time promotion. Use customer feedback and sales data to determine whether the product is worth investing in further.

Keep Your Brand Cohesive:

As you expand your product range, make sure to keep your brand cohesive. This means maintaining a consistent style and messaging across all your product offerings to ensure that they are recognizable as part of your brand.

Stay on Top of Inventory Management:

Expanding your product range can increase your inventory levels, so it's important to stay on top of inventory management to avoid overstocking or running out of stock. Use inventory management software to help you track your stock levels and sales data.

Focus on Marketing:

When introducing new products, it's important to focus on marketing to raise awareness and generate sales. This can involve creating targeted advertising campaigns, leveraging social media platforms, and reaching out to influencers or bloggers to promote your products.

In conclusion, expanding your product range is an important step in growing your Amazon return pallet business. By researching market trends, considering customer needs, sourcing from multiple suppliers, testing new products, keeping your brand cohesive, staying on top of inventory management, and focusing on marketing, you can successfully expand your offerings and increase your revenue streams.

Hiring employees or outsourcing tasks

You might need to think about recruiting staff or outsourcing work as your Amazon return pallet business expands to help manage your burden. The following are some things to take into account when choosing whether to recruit workers or outsource tasks:

Skills and Expertise:

Consider the skills and expertise required for the tasks you need to delegate. Hiring employees can be beneficial if you need someone with specific skills, such as a graphic designer or a marketing specialist. Outsourcing tasks can be more cost-effective if you only need someone to perform a specific task or if you require a skillset that you do not possess.

Cost:

Hiring employees can be more expensive than outsourcing tasks, as you need to consider additional costs such as payroll taxes, benefits, and overhead expenses. Outsourcing tasks, on the other hand, can be more cost-effective as you only pay for the specific task or project without the added expenses of employee benefits.

Flexibility:

Outsourcing tasks can provide more flexibility in terms of scheduling and workload. You can hire freelancers or contract workers on a project basis, allowing you to scale your workforce up or down depending on your needs. Hiring employees can provide more long-term stability but may require more commitment in terms of hours and workload.

Management:

Hiring employees requires more management than outsourcing tasks. You need to provide training and support to employees, as well as manage their performance and development. Outsourcing tasks may require less management, as you are hiring someone who is already skilled in the specific task.

Control:

Hiring employees gives you more control over the work being done, as you can provide more oversight and guidance. Outsourcing tasks can be more challenging in terms of control, as you may not have direct supervision over the person completing the task.

Ultimately, the decision to hire employees or outsource tasks depends on your specific business needs and goals. Consider factors such as skills and expertise required, cost, flexibility, management, and control when making your decision. A combination of both hiring employees and outsourcing tasks may also be a viable option, depending on your business needs.

Scaling up your business for long-term success

Scaling up your Amazon return pallet business is an important step for long-term success. Here are some key strategies to consider as you grow your business:

Build a strong team: As your business grows, you will need a team to help you manage the workload. Hire employees who share your vision for the business and who can help you achieve your goals. Train your team members and delegate tasks as appropriate to ensure that everyone is working efficiently.

Invest in technology: Technology can help you manage your inventory, streamline your operations, and improve customer service. Consider investing in inventory management software, a customer relationship management system, and other tools that can help you grow your business.

Expand your product offering: By adding more products to your range, you may attract more customers and generate more cash. To diversify your business, think about introducing new product categories or finding new sales channels.

Pay attention to customer care: Developing a loyal customer base requires excellent customer service. Inquiries and concerns from customers should be handled quickly, and efforts should be made to go above and beyond. By doing this, you'll enhance your brand's reputation and draw in more clients.

Build relationships with suppliers: As you scale up your business, you will need to work closely with suppliers to ensure that you are getting the best deals on return pallets. Build strong relationships with reputable suppliers and negotiate for better prices and terms as your volume increases.

Develop a marketing plan: A solid marketing plan can help you reach new customers and build your brand. Consider developing a website, running social media ads, and attending trade shows to promote your business.

Stay organized: As your business grows, it can become increasingly challenging to manage your inventory and operations. Develop systems and processes to help you stay organized, and invest in tools and technology that can help you manage your workload efficiently.

In conclusion, meticulous preparation and execution are required when scaling up your Amazon return pallet business. Develop a solid team, spend money on technology, expand your product range, concentrate on customer service, establish connections with suppliers, create a marketing strategy, and maintain organization. You can expand your business and find long-term success if you put the correct plans in place.

Conclusion

Building a successful Amazon return pallet business can be a lucrative opportunity for those willing to invest the time and effort required. Throughout this guide, we have explored various aspects of this business, from finding legitimate suppliers to expanding your product range and scaling up your business for long-term success.

Here are the key takeaways from this guide:

1. Types of products found in return pallets include overstock, shelf pulls, customer returns, and salvage

items. It's important to understand the condition and value of these items to make informed purchasing decisions.

2. Before purchasing return pallets, evaluate potential suppliers and inspect pallets to ensure you're getting a good value for your investment.

3. Sorting products into categories and identifying high-value items can help maximize profits and minimize losses.

4. Choosing the right sales channels and pricing products effectively are key to reaching customers and maximizing profits.

5. Marketing strategies such as social media advertising, email marketing, and attending trade shows can help reach potential customers.

6. Keeping track of inventory is essential to managing a successful business, and using inventory management software can help streamline operations.

7. Reinvesting profits in the business and expanding product offerings can help drive long-term growth.

8. Handling slow-moving inventory and dealing with customer returns and complaints are key challenges that must be addressed.

9. Protecting against scams and fraudulent suppliers is crucial to avoid losses and protect your reputation.

10. As your business grows, it's important to build a strong team, invest in technology, diversify your product line, focus on customer service, build relationships with suppliers, develop a marketing plan, and stay organized.

By following these key takeaways, you can build a successful Amazon return pallet business that is sustainable and profitable over the long term.

Final thoughts on buying and selling Amazon return pallets

In conclusion, buying and selling Amazon return pallets can be a profitable business opportunity for those willing to put in the effort to research, find legitimate suppliers, sort through products, and market their offerings effectively. This guide has provided a comprehensive overview of the many facets involved in running a successful Amazon return pallet business, from identifying high-value items to developing marketing strategies and managing inventory.

It's important to remember that while there are potential profits to be made, there are also risks involved in purchasing return pallets. The condition of the items in the pallets can vary greatly, and it's essential to thoroughly inspect the pallets and evaluate the reputation of potential suppliers before making a purchase.

Additionally, handling slow-moving inventory and dealing with customer returns and complaints can be challenging and time-consuming, but by developing effective strategies for managing these issues, you can minimize losses and maintain a positive reputation.

As with any business, it's important to be flexible and willing to adapt to changing market conditions. This includes expanding your product offerings, diversifying your sales channels, and continually refining your marketing and pricing strategies.

Ultimately, the success of your Amazon return pallet business will depend on a variety of factors, including your ability to identify high-value items, effectively market your products, manage inventory, and maintain strong relationships with suppliers and customers. By following the tips and strategies outlined in this guide, you can build a profitable and sustainable business that provides long-term success and fulfillment.

Encouragement to take action and get started in the business.

You probably want to learn more about this business opportunity if you've read this far about purchasing and selling Amazon return pallets. Although it might seem difficult at first, taking action and getting started is the first step to creating a successful and long-lasting business.

The key to success in this business is to approach it with a mindset of learning and experimentation. As you begin to research potential suppliers, sort through pallets, and market your products, you'll encounter challenges and setbacks along the way. But each of these experiences presents an opportunity to learn and grow, and with persistence and dedication, you can build a thriving business.

The ability to start small and scale up over time as you acquire expertise and confidence is one advantage of this business. Start by buying a few pallets, then try various distribution methods and pricing structures. You can broaden your product offerings and raise your volume of purchases as you learn more about the market and the needs of your customers.

As you expand your business, it's critical to remain inspired and keep a positive attitude. Keep in mind that success requires time to achieve and that it's acceptable to make errors in order to grow. As you go through the ups and downs of entrepreneurship, remember to celebrate small wins along the way and stay focused on your long-term objectives.

In conclusion, for those prepared to put in the needed work and commitment, purchasing and selling Amazon return pallets can be a successful and rewarding business. You can create a prosperous business that offers both long-term financial success and personal fulfillment if you are dedicated to learning, experimenting, and persevering. So instead of waiting longer, why not explore this exciting business opportunity right now?